MOZART

his greatest
PIANO SOLOS

Vol. II

Minuets

Waltzes

Childhood Compositions

Easy Pieces

Variations

Sonatas

Sonatinas

Compiled by
ALEXANDER SHEALY

Sole selling agent: **ASHLEY DEALERS SERVICE** • 263 Veterans Blvd., Carlstadt, N. J. 07072

CONTENTS

First Minuet

Wolfgang Amadeus Mozart

K. 2

Second Minuet

Wolfgang Amadeus Mozart

K. 4

Third Minuet

Wolfgang Amadeus Mozart
K. 5

Waltz in D

Wolfgang Amadeus Mozart
K. 567 No. 4

Allegro moderato.

Waltz in A

Wolfgang Amadeus Mozart

K. 567 No. 5

Waltz in D

Wolfgang Amadeus Mozart

K. 586 No. 6

Allegro moderato.

Minuet and Trio

Wolfgang Amadeus Mozart

Sketchbook: 1764

Romance

(from the Piano Concerto in Dm)

Andante.
cantabile

Wolfgang Amadeus Mozart

K. 466

Two Short Pieces

I.

Wolfgang Amadeus Mozart

Sketchbook: 1764

Two Minuets

I.

Wolfgang Amadeus Mozart
1762

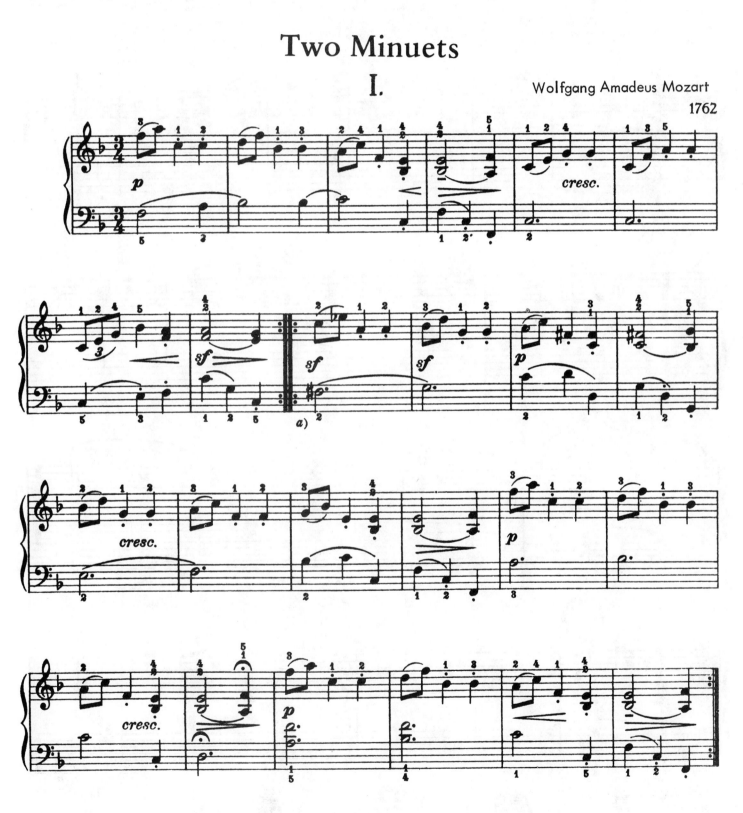

II.

Romance

Wolfgang Amadeus Mozart

K. Anhang 205

a)

Allegro

Wolfgang Amadeus Mozart

K. 312 (189^{i})

Allegro

(Sophie & Konstanze)

Wolfgang Amadeus Mozart

K. 400 (372a)

phie___ Con-stan - ce*)

So-

*Written in by the composer.

Acht Menuette

Komponiert in Salzburg vermutlich 1779

KV 315g

Trio

(Men. d. C.)

(Menuetto)

III

Trio

(Men. d. C.)

(Menuetto)

VI

Trio

(Men. d. C.)

(Menuetto)

VII

Trio

(Men. d. C.)

(Menuetto)

VIII

Trio

(Men. d. C.)

Rondo

on "William of Orange"

TEMA
Allegro

Wolfgang Amadeus Mozart
K. 25

VAR. II

VAR. III

VAR. IV

VAR.VII

THEMES AND VARIATIONS

on a march from Grétry's opera "Mariages Samnites"

Wolfgang Amadeus Mozart
K. 352

VAR. II

VAR.III

VAR. V
Minore

VAR. VI
Maggiore

VAR. VII
Adagio.

VAR. VIII
Allegro

Salve tu, Domine

Wolfgang Amadeus Mozart

K. 398

TEMA

VAR. I

VAR.II

60

61

VAR.VI

Allegretto in A

Wolfgang Amadeus Mozart

K. 137 Anhang

TEMA
Allegretto

VAR.II
Cantabile

VAR.III
Minore

VAR. IV
Maggiore

VAR. V
Adagio

attacca subito:

VAR. VI
Allegro

Sonata in B♭

Wolfgang Amadeus Mozart

K. 498a (Anhang 136)

Andante (♪ = 76)

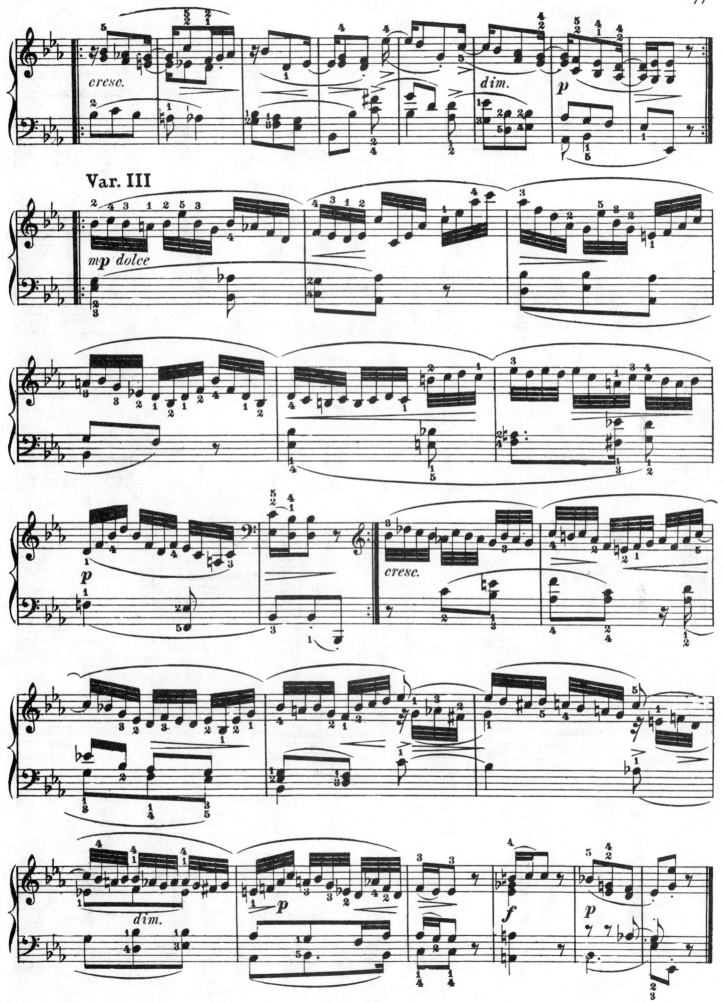

Var. III

Menuetto
Allegretto (♩=144)

a)

Trio

Menuetto D. C.

a)

Rondo
Allegro (♩.= 100)

a)

Tempo Iº

Sonata in F

Wolfgang Amadeus Mozart

K. 533 & K. 494

a)

Rondo

Allegretto ($\downarrow$ = 63)

Minore

Sonata in D

Wolfgang Amadeus Mozart

K. 205b

Rondeau en Polonaise
Andante (♩ = 72)

Tema
Andante (♩ = 120)

Var. III

Var. IV

Var. VII

Minore (♩ = 112)

Var. VIII
Maggiore (♩= 126)

Var. IX

Var. XI
Adagio cantabile ($\flat$ = 92)

Var. XII
Allegro (♩=132)

a)

Sonatina VI in C

Wolfgang Amadeus Mozart
K. 439

Allegro

MENUETTC
Allegretto

Fine

TRIO

Menuetto da capo

Adagio

FINALE
Allegro

Sonata in F

Wolfgang Amadeus Mozart
K. 547a (54 Anh., 135 & 138a)

a)

Close
Final

Allegretto (♩ = 104)

Sonatina I in C

Wolfgang Amadeus Mozart
K. 439

Allegro brillante

MENUETTO
Allegretto

TRIO

Menuetto da capo

Sonatina II in A

MENUETTO
Allegretto

Fine

TRIO

Menuetto da capo

159

RONDO
Allegro

Sonatina III in D

Wolfgang Amadeus Mozart

K. 439

Adagio

MENUETTO
Allegretto

Fine

TRIO

Menuetto da capo

RONDO
Allegro

Sonatina IV in B♭

Wolfgang Amadeus Mozart

K. 439

Andante grazioso

MENUETTO
Allegretto

Menuetto da capo

RONDO
Allegro

Sonatina V in F

Wolfgang Amadeus Mozart

K. 439

Adagio

MENUETTO
Allegro

Fine

TRIO

Menuetto da capo

POLONAISE